Dear Reader,

We all need our own little BLUEPRINTS, or plans, in life. Sometimes making a plan is fun. Sometimes it's hard. Sometimes the plan doesn't work, so we make a new one. And sometimes, the plan is exactly what we need, just when we need it. As you read this Have a Plan Book, we hope you will ask questions, talk about it with family and friends, and create your very own plan. You can do this on your own or together with a grown-up.

Your plan may grow and change each time you read your book, and that's great! As life happens, plans change. But remember, having a little Blueprint is always helpful, in difficult times and in good times. So go ahead: BLUEPRINT IT!

Lovingly,

Your friends at little BLUEPRINT

P.S. Children and adults around the world are making their own little BLUEPRINTS. If you want to see the plans of others, or share yours, just go to

www.littleBLUEPRINT.com

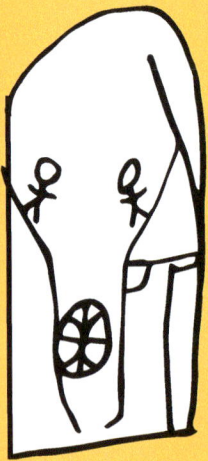

HAVE A PLAN *Books*

To purchase a hardcover or
personalized version of any
little BLUEPRINT book,
with names, optional photo(s),
and details, please go to:

www.littleBLUEPRINT.com

The author would like to thank,
for all of their support and expertise:
Dan Siegel, M.D.;
Nina Shapiro, M.D.; and
my editors, Leslie Budnick and Gina Shaw.
A special thanks to:
Phoebe, age 10, for her blueprint illustration; and
Dylan & Asher, age 7, for their title page illustration.

WHEN MY PARENTS

Divorce,

I HAVE A PLAN

by Katherine Eskovitz

illustrated by Jessica Churchill

I have two parents:

MY MOTHER AND MY FATHER.

They are married.

I can draw or paste a picture of them here.

MY PARENTS ARE GETTING DIVORCED.

Two adults can choose to get married,
and they can choose to
get divorced.

Sometimes parents choose
to end their marriage by
getting divorced because
they feel they will be happier
apart rather than together,
even if it seems harder.

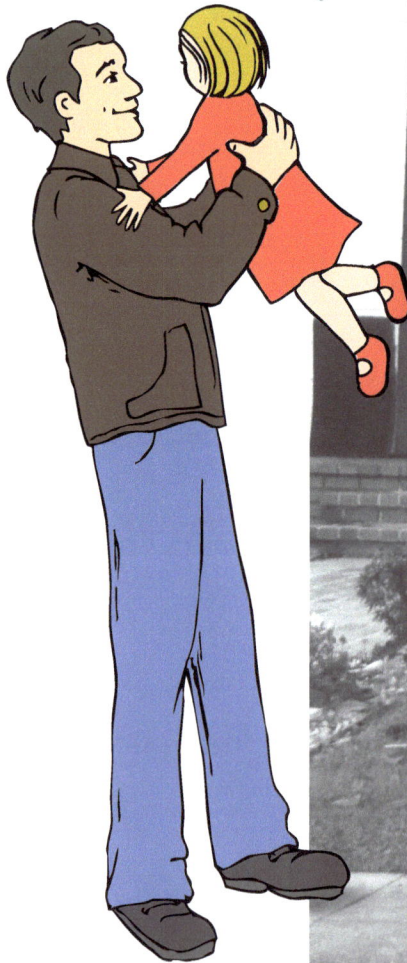

While parents can get divorced from each other,
kids can't get divorced from each other
or from their parents.
BROTHERS AND SISTERS ARE FOREVER,
and so are
PARENTS AND THEIR CHILDREN.

My family will change,
but I will have my family forever.
I am always taken care of, whether my
parents are married or divorced.

MY PARENTS WILL ALWAYS **LOVE** ME,

even if sometimes I see one of my parents
more than the other.

When my parents divorce,

they will no longer live

together in the same home.

They will each have their own home.
Both of their homes will be mine, too.

This means I will have
TWO TOOTHBRUSHES,
TWO PILLOWS,
and
TWO BEDS.

There will be a schedule, and I will go back
and forth to each of my homes.

My parents feel a lot of big emotions about their divorce.

Sometimes they seem sad, angry, tired, or just really busy.

It is hard to see my parents like this.

I feel lots of emotions about my parents' divorce, too: I feel

SAD,

ANGRY,

SCARED,

CONFUSED,

and sometimes I feel nothing at all.

One emotion my parents do **NOT** want me
to feel about their divorce is guilty.
My parents want me to understand that
they decided to divorce, but it has
nothing to do with me, and I am not to blame.
Children are never to blame when
parents get divorced.

When I feel sad or angry about my parents' divorce,

There are things I can do to feel better.

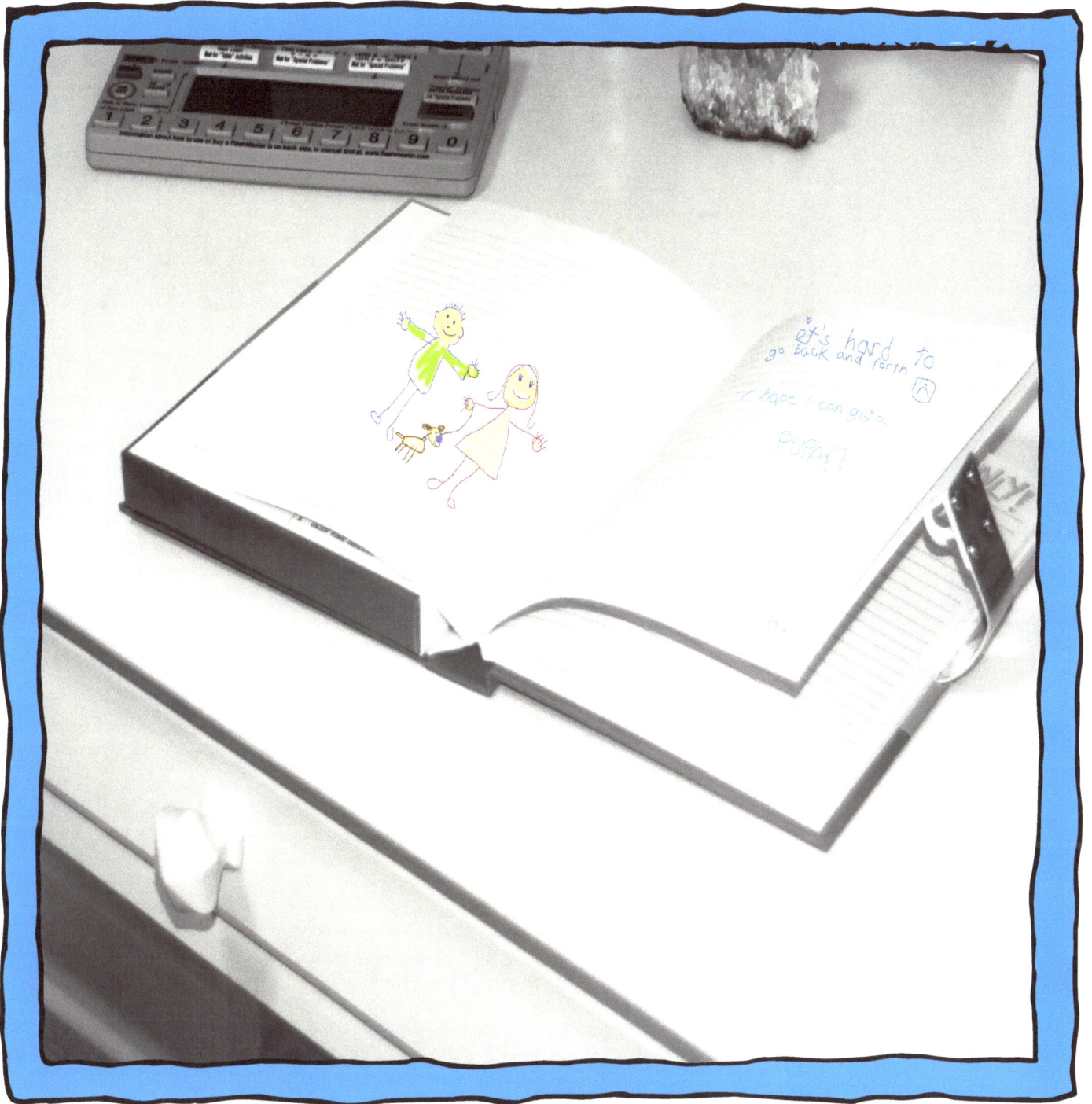

I CAN KEEP A JOURNAL

to write down or draw what's happening and how I feel.

I can talk to my parents about how I feel. I can ask them questions about their divorce and what is going on. I can tell them what I think. I can tell them I want them to get along with each other. I can still mention each of my parents to the other, even when they are divorced.

with each of my parents alone, in each of my homes.

We can have a **FAMILY NOTEBOOK**, and
my parents can write down notes for each other
about me when they don't want to forget something.
They can remind each other of things
I should pack, food I ate, activities we did, or
anything great they want to share about me.
My parents are lucky
they will always get to share me,
and I can help.

I can make a list of the most important things
to remember about my parents' divorce and
hang it up where I will see it.
For example, I can remind myself:

1. My parents love me, and they always will.
2. Their divorce is not my fault.
3. My family changes, but family is forever.
4. Some of the changes from my parents' divorce are good.
   My parents will be happier, even if it can be difficult, and
   I will have more special time with each of my parents alone.
5. I have friends, family, and professionals (doctor, counselor)
   I can talk to when I am sad or have questions.
6. Other things in my life stay the same:
   I have the same friends, activities, and interests.
7. It is ok to feel sad, angry, or confused about their divorce.
   It takes time to get used to divorce.

I CAN WRITE DOWN MY SCHEDULE

to remember when I will be at each of my homes

so I will always know on what day I will be where.

I CAN KEEP SPECIAL THINGS

—a stuffed animal and pictures—
in each of my homes and help
decorate my rooms.

My Plan
1. Pick out something special for each room.
2. Get a Family Journal.
3. Write in my own journal about how I feel.

I CAN START TO FEEL BETTER by making my own plan to deal with my parents' divorce.

Here is MY PLAN

Check out other children's BLUEPRINTS from around the world and share yours, too!

Other titles in the
HAVE A PLAN Series

WHEN IT'S TIME FOR BED, I HAVE A PLAN

TO CELEBRATE THE HOLIDAYS, I HAVE A PLAN

WHEN I MISS SOMEONE SPECIAL, I HAVE A PLAN

WHEN I MISS MY SPECIAL PET, I HAVE A PLAN

TO BE SAFE AT HOME, I HAVE A PLAN

TO BE SAFE ON THE GO, I HAVE A PLAN

TO KEEP MY BODY SAFE, I HAVE A PLAN

TO BE A HEALTHY EATER, I HAVE A PLAN

WHEN MY PARENTS SEPARATE, I HAVE A PLAN

AND MORE

New titles added regularly at

www.littleBLUEPRINT.com

All titles are available ready-made and personalized

playground   School   Home

little
BLUEPRINT
Empowering children. Training the brain.
WWW.LITTLEBLUEPRINT.COM

www.ingramcontent.com/pod-product-compliance
Lightning Source LLC
LaVergne TN
LVHW072101070426
835508LV00002B/215